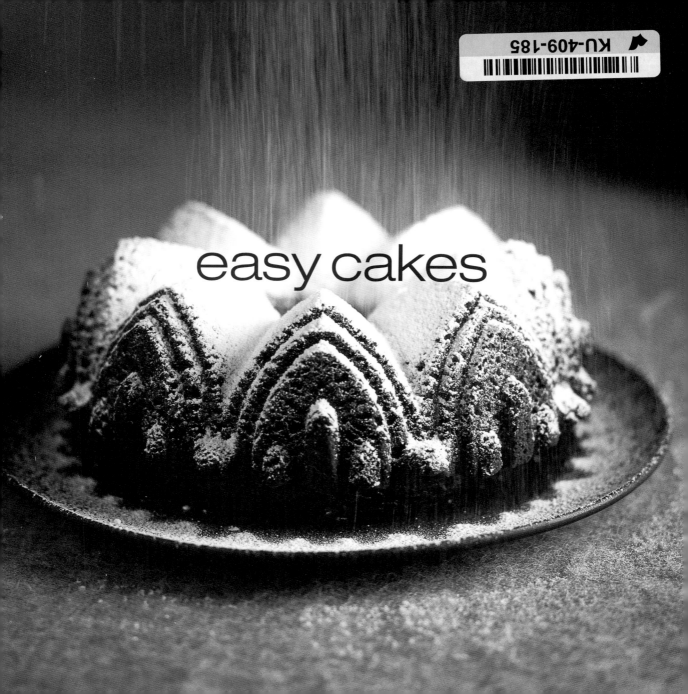

easy cakes

RYLAND
PETERS
& SMALL

LONDON NEW YORK

easy cakes

Linda Collister

photography by Diana Miller

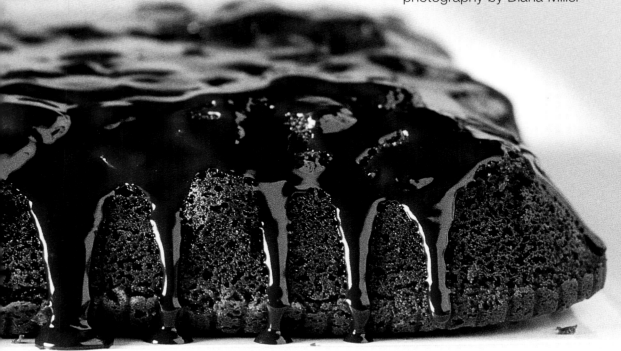

First published in Great Britain in 2004
by Ryland Peters & Small
20–21 Jockey's Fields
London WC1R 4BW
www.rylandpeters.com

10 9 8 7 6 5 4 3 2

Text © Linda Collister 2004
Design and photographs
© Ryland Peters & Small 2004

Printed in China

ISBN 978 1 84172 712 7

A CIP record for this book is available
from the British Library.

Dedication
To my lovely in-laws.

Acknowledgements
I would to thank the many people who
helped with this book; Elsa Petersen-
Schepelern, Steve Painter, Diana Miller,
Bridget Sargeson, Vicky Keppel-
Compton, Róisín Nield, Barbara Levy,
Simon Silverwood, Shelley Rau, Annette
and Will Hertz, Alan Hertz, Robert
Carmack and Michelle Kershaw.

Senior Designer Steve Painter
Commissioning Editor
   Elsa Petersen-Schepelern
Production Patricia Harrington
Art Director Gabriella Le Grazie
Publishing Director Alison Starling

Food Stylist Bridget Sargeson
Stylist Róisín Nield

Notes
• All spoon measurements are level
unless otherwise specified.
• All eggs are large unless otherwise
specified. Uncooked or partly cooked
eggs should not be served to the very
young, the very old, those with
compromised immune systems or
to pregnant women.
• Before baking, weigh or measure all
ingredients exactly and prepare baking
tins or sheets.
• Ovens should be preheated to the
specified temperature. Recipes in this
book were tested in several kinds of
oven – all work slightly differently.
I recommend using an oven thermometer
and consulting the maker's handbook for
special instructions.

contents

a piece of cake ...

'A piece of cake' is something simple, and here is a collection of pieces of cake: easy to make, great to look at, delicious to eat.

The keys to good cake baking are not complex recipes or great skill; the keys are practice, care and good, fresh ingredients. Unless you have a patisserie or a farmers' market on your doorstep, no cake you buy will be as delicious as one you bake yourself. Fresh, free-range eggs, real unsalted butter, true vanilla, good chocolate, fresh nuts and spices, and quality dried fruit give flavour that can't be beaten.

How can you make baking easy? First, get to know your equipment. Turn on the oven well in advance so it is thoroughly heated and ready for the cake; some ovens take 15 minutes to reach the correct temperature. Ovens vary and thermostats can be unreliable, so check the temperature with an oven thermometer. Some fan ovens also recommend a slightly lower oven temperature.

An electric mixer is invaluable for beating, whisking and mixing; it will save you a lot of time and energy. For effective mixing, ingredients should be at room temperature, unless the recipe says otherwise. Don't forget to scrape down the bowl from time to time.

When you buy cake tins, read the maker's notes carefully – some tins have special coatings which need particular treatment. Because they will bake faster, they should be used at a lower oven temperature or for less time. Look out for good-quality tins with non-stick coatings, and use pre-cut or ready-made paper liners. If you brush inside the tin with melted unsalted butter, unmoulding the cake after baking will be no problem.

Home baking is a great European tradition, and cakes are an important part of it. They include delicate, airy sponges of France and Italy; sweet, enriched, fruit-flecked bread doughs from Germany and the heart of Europe; hearty fruit cakes from Britain and Ireland; and rich spice cakes from Scandinavia. Each wave of emigrants to North America took along their favourite recipes and ingredients as well as cooking tins. The Bundt tin, now the quintessential American cake tin, started out in Central Europe a couple of hundred years ago when bakers put a metal tube in the centre of their large, deep, cake moulds to help the middle bake more evenly and let it rise higher. These developed into the elaborate kugelhopf moulds still used in Alsace, and the huge range and fancy, detailed designs of heavy, metal Bundt tins.

Finally, a word about coffee cakes. Until I married an American, I thought these were sponge cakes flavoured with real coffee. Now I know this ain't necessarily so. For my husband, coffee cake is a cake accompanied by a cup of coffee at any time of the day – breakfast, mid-morning, mid-afternoon – or as a pudding. This tradition comes from Germany and Central Europe. There, even the simplest meal was concluded with, or consisted of, coffee and a sweet bake. What civilized people!

layer cakes

If you can make muffins, you can make this cake. It is really a rich chocolate chip muffin recipe, so just measure and mix. The icing is a simple butter icing made with cocoa.

triple chocolate layer cake

450 g self-raising flour

60 g cocoa powder

a good pinch of salt

400 g caster sugar

225 ml sunflower oil

2 large eggs, beaten

225 ml milk

1 teaspoon real vanilla extract

150 g chocolate chips
or chopped plain chocolate,
plus extra to decorate

icing

125 g unsalted butter,
at room temperature

330 g icing sugar, sieved

6 tablespoons
cocoa powder, sieved

4 tablespoons milk

½ teaspoon vanilla

*3 sandwich tins, 20 cm diameter,
greased and base-lined*

one 3-layer cake

To make the sponge, sift the flour, cocoa, salt and sugar into a large bowl, and make a hollow in the centre. Pour the oil, beaten eggs, milk and vanilla into the hollow in the dry ingredients, and mix gradually with a wooden spoon. Add the chocolate chips and stir well. Divide the mixture between the 3 prepared tins.

Bake in a preheated oven at 180°C (350°F) Gas 4 for 20–25 minutes or until a skewer inserted in the centre comes out clean. Let the cakes cool in the tins for 5 minutes, then carefully turn out onto a wire rack to cool completely.

Meanwhile, to make the icing, put the soft butter in a bowl and, using a wooden spoon or an electric mixer, beat until very creamy. Gradually beat in the icing sugar, cocoa, milk and vanilla to make a thick, smooth icing.

When the cakes are completely cold, use the icing to layer them. Spread about one-sixth of the icing on the top of one cake. Gently set a second cake on top and spread with another one-sixth of the icing. Top with the last cake, then coat the top and sides with the rest of the icing. Decorate with extra chocolate chips.

Store in an airtight container and eat within 4 days.

An elegant, mile-high, three-layer sponge cake, feather-light but full of rich flavours. Instead of the maple syrup icing, you can use Maple Cream (page 61).

maple syrup pecan cake

350 g unsalted butter, at room temperature

280 g caster sugar

4 large eggs, lightly beaten

3 tablespoons pure maple syrup

120 g pecan nuts, finely chopped (in a food processor), but not ground

350 g self-raising flour, sieved

a pinch of salt

icing

225 ml pure maple syrup

2 large egg whites

pecan halves, to decorate

a rubber spatula

3 sandwich tins, 20 cm diameter, greased and base-lined

makes one 3-layer cake

Using an electric mixer, beat the butter until lighter in colour, then add the sugar, a spoonful at a time, while still beating. When all the sugar has been added, scrape down the sides of the bowl, then beat until the mixture is very light and fluffy. Beat in the eggs a spoonful at a time, then gradually beat in the maple syrup. Add the pecans, flour and salt to the bowl and, using a large metal spoon or rubber spatula, gently fold into the mixture.

Divide the mixture between the 3 prepared tins and spread evenly. Bake in a preheated oven at 180°C (350°F) Gas 4 for 25–30 minutes, until the cakes are golden and springy to the touch. Let cool for a minute, then run a round-bladed knife around the inside edge of the tins to loosen the sponges and carefully turn out onto a wire rack to cool completely.

Meanwhile, to make the icing, heat the maple syrup in a medium, heavy pan and let boil gently until it reaches 115°C (238°F) on a sugar thermometer (softball stage) – 5 minutes if you don't have a thermometer. Take care, because the syrup can bubble up and boil over if the heat is too high. While the syrup is heating, whisk the egg whites until stiff peaks form using an electric mixer or whisk. Pour the hot syrup onto the egg whites in a thin stream while still whisking constantly. Keep whisking for a further 1 minute or until the icing is very thick and fluffy.

When the cakes are completely cold, use the icing to layer them. Spread about one-sixth of the mixture on top of one cake. Gently set a second cake on top and spread with another one-sixth of the icing. Top with the last cake, then coat the top and sides with the rest of the icing. Decorate with pecan halves.

This cake is very delicate – it cuts best the next day. Store at room temperature in an airtight container. Best eaten within 4 days.

A weird but wonderfully exotic recipe from Australia – a moist, fresh fruit cake packed with flavour. Use a small fresh pineapple or a carton of ready-prepared fresh pineapple. Leave plain, or decorate with dried banana chips or glacé pineapple chunks.

fresh pineapple layer cake

200 g prepared fresh pineapple

180 g peeled ripe bananas (about 2 small)

250 g self-raising flour

½ teaspoon baking powder

a good pinch of salt

½ teaspoon ground cinnamon

a good pinch of freshly grated nutmeg

225 g light muscovado sugar

2 large eggs, beaten

225 ml sunflower oil

icing

175 g cream cheese

50 g unsalted butter, at room temperature

150 g icing sugar, sieved

1 tablespoon lemon juice

2 sandwich tins, 20 cm diameter, greased and base-lined

makes one 2-layer cake

Put the pineapple in a food processor and blend until fairly finely chopped, or chop with a knife, saving all the juice. Mash the bananas coarsely with a fork.

Sift the flour, baking powder, salt, cinnamon and nutmeg into a large bowl. Mix in the sugar, then make a hollow in the centre. Put the prepared pineapple and bananas, eggs and oil in the hollow, then mix all the ingredients together with a wooden spoon. When thoroughly mixed, divide between the 2 prepared tins and spread evenly.

Bake in a preheated oven at 180°C (350°F) Gas 4 for 30–35 minutes until firm to the touch. Leave for a minute, then run a knife around the inside of the tin to loosen the sponge. Turn out onto a wire rack to cool completely.

To make the icing, beat the cream cheese and butter with an electric mixer or whisk. Using low speed, beat in the icing sugar, 1 tablespoon at a time. Add lemon juice to taste.

Use the icing to layer the cakes. Spread about half the icing on top of one cake. Gently set the second cake on top, then coat the top and sides with the remaining icing. Serve at room temperature.

Store in an airtight container in a cool cupboard or the refrigerator and eat within 4 days.

A simple vanilla sponge filled with whipped cream, good vanilla fudge (homemade or from a specialist shop) and sliced bananas. If you prefer a cake that doesn't need to be kept in the refrigerator, use the Toffee Topping (page 61). Real fudge fans can decorate the cake with small pieces of extra fudge.

banana fudge layer cake

175 g unsalted butter, softened

150 g caster sugar

25 g light muscovado sugar

3 large eggs, at room temperature, beaten

175 g self-raising flour

½ teaspoon real vanilla extract

1 tablespoon milk

filling and icing

300 ml whipping cream, chilled

125 g vanilla fudge, chilled

2 ripe medium bananas, thinly sliced

extra fudge, to decorate, (optional)

3 sandwich tins, 20 cm diameter, greased and base-lined

makes one 3-layer cake

To make the sponge, put the butter, caster and muscovado sugars, beaten eggs, flour, vanilla and milk in a large bowl. Beat at medium speed with an electric mixer or whisk until smooth and thoroughly blended. Divide the mixture between the 3 prepared tins and spread evenly.

Bake in a preheated oven at 180°C (350°F) Gas 4 for about 20 minutes, until just firm to the touch. Let cool for a minute, then run a round-bladed knife inside the rim of the tin just to loosen the sponges. Turn out onto a wire rack and let cool completely.

When ready to assemble, put the cream in a chilled bowl and whip until soft peaks form. Grate the fudge onto the cream and gently stir in. Set one layer of sponge on a serving platter, spread with a third of the cream and cover with half the banana slices. Top with another layer of sponge and spread with half the remaining cream, top with the rest of the bananas, then finally add the last layer of sponge. Spread the remaining cream on top of the cake.

Keep cool and eat the same day, or store in an airtight container in the refrigerator and eat within 2 days.

A good cake for a party, this one looks wonderful and cuts easily. The vanilla sponge is baked in a rectangular tin, cut into two strips, then sandwiched with jam and topped with whipped cream and fresh berries.

raspberries-and-cream layer cake

230 g unsalted butter, softened

230 g caster sugar

4 large eggs, at room temperature, beaten

½ teaspoon vanilla essence

1 tablespoon milk

230 g self-raising flour

½ teaspoon baking powder

filling and topping

5–6 tablespoons Fresh Raspberry (or strawberry) Preserve (page 62)

225 ml double cream, chilled

450 g small raspberries

a non-stick rectangular cake tin, 27 x 18 cm, or a roasting tin, greased

makes one 2-layer cake

To make the sponge, put the butter in a large bowl, then add the sugar, eggs, vanilla, milk, flour and baking powder. Beat with an electric mixer or whisk using medium speed. When very smooth and thoroughly blended, spoon the mixture into the prepared cake tin and spread evenly, right into the corners.

Bake in a preheated oven at 180°C (350°F) Gas 4 for about 25 minutes, or until the sponge just springs back when gently pressed in the centre. Remove the tin from the oven and let cool for 10 minutes before turning out onto a wire rack to cool completely.

With a large, sharp knife or bread knife trim off the edges, then cut the sponge in half down its length to make 2 long strips.

Set 1 strip on a serving platter, then spread with the preserve. Top with the second layer of sponge and press down gently. Whip the cream until very thick and soft peaks form, then spread over the top of the cake. Decorate with berries and serve.

Store in an airtight container in the refrigerator and eat within 3 days.

bundt cakes

Serve warm with Toffee Sauce (page 61) for a real treat.

The moist texture comes from the cold puréed apples.

chocolate spice cake

150 g plain flour

50 g cocoa powder

½ teaspoon baking powder

1 teaspoon bicarbonate of soda

a pinch of salt

1 teaspoon ground cinnamon

1 teaspoon ground ginger

200 g light muscovado sugar

50 ml sunflower oil

2 large eggs, beaten

150 ml sour cream

75 ml unsweetened apple purée

3 tablespoons chopped crystallized stem ginger

icing sugar, for dusting

Toffee Topping or Toffee Sauce (page 61), to serve

a Bundt tin, 23 cm diameter, well greased, or a 900 g loaf tin, greased and lined

makes one Bundt cake or loaf cake

Sift the flour, cocoa, baking powder, bicarbonate of soda, salt, cinnamon and ground ginger into a large bowl. Mix in the sugar and make a hollow in the centre.

Put the oil, eggs, sour cream and apple purée in another bowl and whisk well. Add to the hollow in the dry ingredients and stir gently until thoroughly mixed. Stir in the stem ginger.

Pour into the prepared tin and bake in a preheated oven at 180°C (350°F) Gas 4 for about 45 minutes, or until a skewer inserted in the thickest part of the cake comes out clean.

Let cool in the tin for 20 minutes, then turn out onto a wire rack to cool completely.

Serve at room temperature dusted with icing sugar or topped with Toffee Topping (page 61) or warm with Toffee Sauce or whipped cream.

Store in an airtight container and eat within 5 days.

Plain chocolate and white chocolate in one rich attractive cake. Serve with chocolate sauce or whipped cream.

double chocolate ripple

250 g unsalted butter, at room temperature

250 g caster sugar

4 large eggs, at room temperature

a good pinch of salt

1 teaspoon real vanilla extract

250 g self-raising flour

75 g plain chocolate, chopped

75 g best-quality white chocolate, chopped

1 tablespoon cocoa powder

icing sugar, for dusting

a Bundt tin, 23 cm diameter, greased, or a 900 g loaf tin, greased and base-lined

makes one Bundt cake or loaf cake

Put the butter in an electric mixer and beat until creamy. Increase the speed and gradually beat in the sugar. Lightly beat the eggs, salt and vanilla in a jug, then add to the creamed mixture, about 1 tablespoon at a time, beating well after each addition. Add 1 tablespoon of the flour with the last 2 portions of egg to prevent the mixture from separating.

Sift the rest of the flour onto the mixture and gently fold in with a large metal spoon.

Spoon half the mixture into another bowl.

Put the plain chocolate in a heatproof bowl set over a saucepan of steaming water and melt it gently. Remove the bowl and let cool while you melt the white chocolate in the same way.

Sift the cocoa onto 1 bowl of the cake mixture, add the cooled melted plain chocolate and mix gently. Using a clean metal spoon, stir the melted white chocolate into the other bowl of cake mixture.

Spoon both mixtures into the tin, adding each mixture alternately. To make the marbling, draw a knife through the mixtures and swirl together.

Bake in a preheated oven at 180°C (350°F) Gas 4 for about 50 minutes or until a skewer inserted in the thickest part of the cake comes out clean. Let cool for 20 minutes, then turn out onto a wire rack to cool completely. Serve dusted with icing sugar.

Store in an airtight container and eat within 5 days.

Note If using a loaf tin, bake at the same temperature for 1¼ hours.

Elegant enough to serve for a dinner party with whipped cream or Chocolate Fudge Sauce (page 61) – or make as a batch of muffins to take to work.

hazelnut chocolate mini cakes

200 g ready-skinned (white) hazelnuts

6 large egg whites

150 g plain flour

45 g cocoa powder

200 g icing sugar

50 g light muscovado sugar

175 g unsalted butter, melted and cooled

a mini Bundt tin or 12-hole muffin tray, lined with paper cases

makes 6 small Bundt cakes or 12 muffins

Put the nuts in a baking dish and toast in a preheated oven at 150°C (300°F) Gas 2 until a good even golden brown, about 15 minutes. Cool, then transfer to a processor and pulse to make a fairly fine powder. Increase the oven heat to 200°C (400°F) Gas 6.

Put the egg whites in a spotlessly clean, grease-free bowl and whisk until soft peaks form. Sift the flour, cocoa, icing sugar and muscovado sugar onto the egg whites. Add the ground hazelnuts and cooled melted butter and gently fold all the ingredients together with a large metal spoon.

Spoon the cake mixture into the tin or muffin tray to fill evenly. Bake in the heated oven for 20 minutes until firm to the touch. Let cool in the tin for 5 minutes, then gently turn out onto a wire rack to cool completely.

Store in an airtight container and eat within 3 days.

An old-fashioned coffee cake, designed to serve with a cup of coffee (not made with it), with plenty of crunchy nut streusel.

traditional pecan coffee cake

streusel

100 g finely chopped pecan nuts

4 tablespoons dark muscovado sugar

1½ teaspoons ground cinnamon

batter

250 g unsalted butter, at room temperature

2 large eggs, at room temperature, beaten

150 g caster sugar

225 ml sour cream

300 g plain flour

½ teaspoon bicarbonate of soda

2 teaspoons baking powder

a good pinch of salt

icing sugar, for dusting

a Bundt tin, 23 cm diameter, well greased, or a 900 g loaf tin, greased and lined

a rubber spatula

makes one Bundt cake or loaf cake

Make the streusel topping mixture first. Mix the pecans, sugar and cinnamon in small bowl and set aside.

To make the batter, put the butter, eggs, sugar and sour cream in a large bowl and beat with an electric mixer on medium speed until smooth and well blended.

Sift the flour, bicarbonate of soda, baking powder and salt onto the mixture and mix in gently.

Spoon half the batter into the tin and spread it evenly with a rubber spatula. Sprinkle with half of the streusel mixture. Spoon the rest of the batter into the tin and spread evenly. Sprinkle with the remaining streusel, then gently press the mixture onto the surface of the batter with the back of a spoon.

Bake in a preheated oven at 180°C (350°F) Gas 4 for 45–55 minutes or until a skewer inserted in the thickest part of the cake comes out clean. Remove the tin from the oven and let cool in the tin, on a wire cooling rack. Let cool completely, then invert onto a serving platter. Dust with icing sugar before serving.

Store in an airtight container and eat within 4 days.

American chef Robert Carmack makes this unusually flavoured pound cake for Christmas and New Year parties, replacing the milk with brandy or bourbon.

festive fruit and nut pound cake

230 g unsalted butter, at room temperature

230 g caster sugar

4 large eggs, at room temperature

3 tablespoons milk, brandy or bourbon

½ teaspoon real vanilla extract

75 g mixed raisins and sultanas

100 g pecan nuts, coarsely chopped

230 g self-raising flour

a pinch of salt

¼ teaspoon ground mace

¼ teaspoon freshly grated nutmeg

icing sugar, for dusting

a Bundt tin, 23 cm diameter, well greased, or 900 g loaf tin, greased and lined

makes one Bundt cake or loaf cake

Put the butter and sugar in a bowl and, using an electric mixer or whisk, beat well until light and fluffy. Break the eggs into a jug, add the milk (or brandy or bourbon) and vanilla and mix with a fork. Gradually beat into the butter mixture, about 1 tablespoon at a time, beating well after each addition.

Put the fruit and pecans in a bowl, add 1 tablespoon of the weighed flour and toss gently.

Sift the remaining flour, salt, mace and nutmeg onto the creamed mixture and gently fold in with a large metal spoon. Add the fruit and pecans to the cake mixture and stir gently. Transfer to the prepared tin and spread evenly.

Bake in a preheated oven at 180°C (350°F) Gas 4 for 45–50 minutes, or until a skewer inserted in the thickest part of the cake comes out clean. Let cool in the tin, then turn out onto a wire rack to cool completely. Serve dusted with icing sugar. Best eaten the next day.

Store in an airtight container and eat within 5 days.

As coffee cakes go, this recipe seems rather plain and simple, but the flavour is superb. Serve for dinner with whipped cream.

whiskey coffee cake
with sultanas and sour cream

batter

50 g sultanas

2 tablespoons Irish whiskey or orange juice

175 g unsalted butter, at room temperature

225 g light muscovado sugar

2 tablespoons maple syrup

4 large eggs, at room temperature, beaten

400 g plain flour

½ teaspoon bicarbonate of soda

2 teaspoons baking powder

a good pinch of salt

125 ml sour cream

glaze

4 tablespoons Irish whiskey or orange juice

4 tablespoons maple syrup

a Bundt tin, 23 cm diameter, well greased, or a 900 g loaf tin, greased and lined

a rubber spatula

makes one Bundt cake or loaf cake

Put the sultanas and whiskey in a small bowl, stir and set aside while you make the rest of the batter.

Put the butter, sugar and maple syrup in a large bowl and beat on high speed with an electric mixer or whisk until light and fluffy. Gradually add the eggs, beating well after each addition.

Sift the flour, bicarbonate of soda, baking powder and salt into the bowl. Add the sour cream, soaked sultanas and whiskey and gently mix all the ingredients with a large metal spoon.

Spoon into the prepared tin and spread evenly with a rubber spatula. Bake in a preheated oven at 180°C (350°F) Gas 4 for 50–60 minutes or until a skewer inserted in the thickest part of the cake comes out clean. Remove the tin from the oven and stand on a wire cooling rack. Let cool for 20 minutes while you make the glaze.

Put the whiskey and maple syrup in a small saucepan and heat gently. Invert the tin onto a deep plate, lift off the tin, then spoon the glaze over the warm cake. Let cool completely.

Store in an airtight container and eat within 4 days.

An old recipe combining dried dates and walnuts for a well-textured, moist cake.

spiced date sour cream coffee cake

200 g pitted dates

175 ml boiling water

200 g unsalted butter, at room temperature

280 g dark muscovado sugar

3 large eggs, at room temperature, beaten

450 g plain flour

1½ teaspoons bicarbonate of soda

2 teaspoons baking powder

1 teaspoon freshly grated nutmeg

½ teaspoon ground cloves or allspice

½ teaspoon ground cinnamon

a good pinch of salt

225 ml sour cream

75 g walnut pieces

icing sugar, for dusting

a Bundt tin, 23 cm diameter, well greased, or a 900 g loaf tin, greased and lined

a rubber spatula

makes one Bundt cake or loaf cake

Put the dates and boiling water in a food processor and pulse or process very briefly to make a coarse purée. Let cool while you make the rest of the batter.

Put the butter and sugar in a large bowl and beat with an electric mixer or whisk until very light in colour and texture. Gradually add the eggs, beating well after each addition.

Sift the flour, bicarbonate of soda, baking powder, nutmeg, cloves, cinnamon and salt into the bowl. Add the sour cream, the cooled date mixture and walnuts and gently mix with a large metal spoon or rubber spatula.

Spoon into the prepared tin and spread evenly using the spatula.

Bake in a preheated oven at 180°C (350°F) Gas 4 for 50–60 minutes or until a skewer inserted in the thickest part of the cake comes out clean. Remove from the oven and let cool, still in the tin, on a wire rack for 20 minutes. Carefully turn out onto the rack to cool completely. Dust with icing sugar before serving.

Store in an airtight tin and eat within 5 days.

A good cake for breakfast or for dinner, served with Toffee Sauce (page 61) or whipped cream.

mini gingerbreads

230 g self-raising flour

1 teaspoon bicarbonate of soda

1 tablespoon ground ginger

1 teaspoon ground mixed spice

¼ teaspoon freshly grated nutmeg

¼ teaspoon ground cloves

115 g unsalted butter, diced

115 g black treacle

115 g golden syrup

115 g dark muscovado sugar

280 ml milk

1 large egg, beaten

a mini Bundt tin, greased, or a 900 g loaf tin, greased and lined

makes 6 small Bundt cakes or one loaf cake

Sift the flour, bicarbonate of soda, ginger, mixed spice, nutmeg and cloves onto a sheet of paper, then tip into a food processor. Add the butter and process until the mixture looks like very fine crumbs.

Put the treacle, golden syrup, sugar and milk in a pan and heat gently until the sugar dissolves. Cool until lukewarm, then, with the processor on, pour the mixture through the feed tube. Add the egg in the same way and process until just thoroughly mixed.

Spoon the mixture into the prepared Bundt tin until the holes are equally filled (or pour into the loaf tin) and bake in a preheated oven at 180°C (350°F) Gas 4 for 20 minutes until firm to the touch.

Let cool for 15 minutes before unmoulding onto a wire rack.

Store in an airtight container and eat within 5 days.

Note If using a loaf tin, bake in a preheated oven at 180°C (350°F) Gas 4 for 45–60 minutes or until a skewer inserted in the centre comes out clean.

This is a cake with plenty of flavour, but not too sweet or rich. The creamy topping can be served separately.

well-spiced carrot cake

250 g self-raising flour

1 teaspoon baking powder

2 teaspoons ground cinnamon

1 teaspoon ground ginger

½ teaspoon freshly grated nutmeg

110 g light muscovado sugar

175 ml sunflower oil

3 large eggs

300 g grated carrots, about 5 medium

50 g walnut or pecan pieces

mascarpone lemon cream

200 g mascarpone cheese

50 g icing sugar, sieved

1 tablespoon lemon juice

extra nuts, to decorate

a Bundt tin, 23 cm diameter, well greased, or a 900 g loaf tin, greased and lined

makes one Bundt cake or loaf cake

Sift the flour, baking powder, cinnamon, ginger, nutmeg and sugar into a large bowl. Make a hollow in the centre.

Put the oil and eggs in a jug, whisk until well mixed, then pour into the hollow in the dry ingredients. Mix well with a wooden spoon, then stir in the grated carrots and nuts.

Transfer the mixture to the prepared tin and spread evenly. Bake in a preheated oven at 180°C (350°F) Gas 4 for 45–55 minutes or until a skewer inserted in the thickest part of the cake comes out clean. Let cool for 15 minutes, then turn out onto a wire rack to cool completely.

To make the topping, mix the mascarpone with the icing sugar, then stir in the lemon juice.

Decorate the top of the cake with some of the topping, then add the nuts. Serve the rest of the mascarpone lemon cream separately.

Store in an airtight container in a very cool place or the refrigerator and eat within 4 days.

For best texture, use fine cornmeal or regular polenta rather than instant polenta. A mild fruity oil will give the best flavour.

italian lemon pistachio miniature cakes

2 large eggs, at room temperature

130 g caster sugar

freshly grated zest of 1 large unwaxed lemon

175 ml milk (or 85 ml each of milk and Marsala)

175 ml virgin olive oil

150 g plain flour

25 g polenta

1 tablespoon baking powder

a pinch of salt

50 g pistachio nuts, coarsely chopped

icing sugar, for dusting

a mini Bundt tin, greased, or a 12-hole muffin tray, lined with paper cases

makes 6 mini Bundt cakes or 12 muffins

Put the eggs and sugar in a large bowl and whisk with an electric mixer or whisk until very thick and pale. On low speed, whisk in the lemon zest, followed by the milk (or milk and Marsala) and olive oil.

Sift the flour, polenta, baking powder and salt onto the mixture and gently fold into the batter with a large metal spoon. When there are no more streaks of flour to be seen, mix in the nuts, then transfer to the prepared tin. Spread evenly, then bake in a preheated oven at 200°C (400°F) Gas 6 for about 20 minutes or until springy when pressed.

Let cool in the tin for 5 minutes, then turn out onto a wire rack to cool completely. Dust with icing sugar before serving with coffee or with fresh fruit and whipped cream or mascarpone lemon cream (page 35).

Store in an airtight container and eat within 2 days.

This cake made with fresh (or defrosted) cranberries has been a Thanksgiving favourite since I first tasted it at a New England Cranberry Festival.

thanksgiving cranberry bundt

filling

60 g whole blanched almonds

150 g fresh cranberries

2 teaspoons ground cinnamon

85 g light muscovado sugar

batter

110 g unsalted butter, at room temperature

2 large eggs, at room temperature, beaten

160 g light muscovado sugar

225 ml sour cream

40 g finely chopped almonds

325 g plain flour

1 teaspoon ground cinnamon

½ teaspoon bicarbonate of soda

1 teaspoon baking powder

icing sugar, for dusting

a Bundt tin, 23 cm diameter, well greased, or a 900 g loaf tin, greased and lined

makes one Bundt cake or loaf cake

Make the filling first. Put the almonds into a food processor and chop finely to make a very coarse powder (rather than using bought finely ground almonds). Transfer to a large bowl.

Put the cranberries in the processor and chop coarsely. Add to the almonds, then add the cinnamon and sugar and mix well. Set aside.

To make the batter, put the soft butter, beaten eggs, sugar, sour cream and chopped almonds in another large bowl. Beat with an electric mixer or whisk on medium speed until very smooth. Sift the flour, cinnamon, bicarbonate of soda and baking powder onto the mixture, then stir in with a large metal spoon. When thoroughly mixed, spoon half the batter into the prepared tin. Sprinkle the cranberry mixture over the batter, then top with the rest of the batter.

Bake in a preheated oven at 180°C (350°F) Gas 4 for about 50 minutes or until a skewer inserted in the thickest part of the cake comes out clean. Let cool in the tin for 15 minutes, then carefully turn out onto a wire rack, dust with icing sugar and let cool completely.

Store in an airtight container and eat within 4 days.

Blueberry Variation In summer, use fresh blueberries for a fresh fruit Bundt. Make the batter as in the main recipe, but omit the cinnamon and add the grated zest of ½ unwaxed lemon.

To make the filling, mix 200 g fresh blueberries with 85 g light muscovado sugar, 60 g chopped almonds and the grated zest of ½ unwaxed lemon. Proceed as in the main recipe.

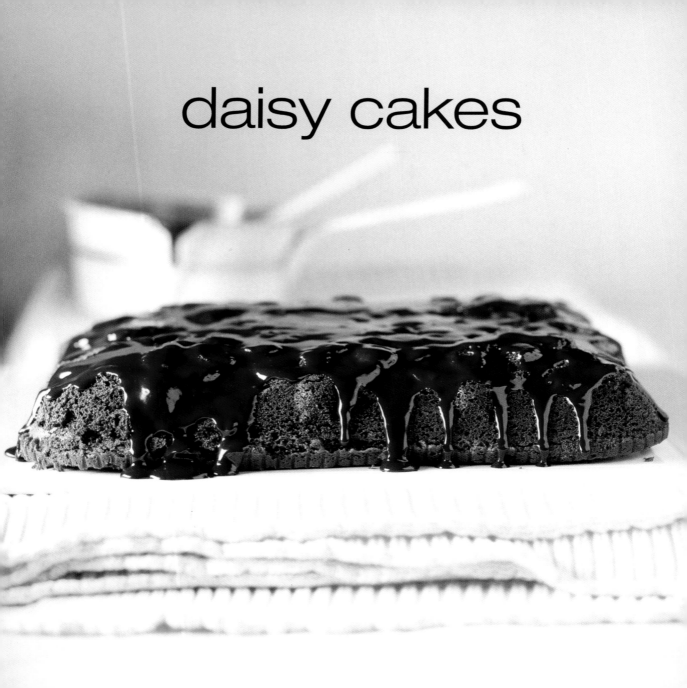

daisy cakes

This may seem a strange way to make a cake, but the final result is a rich, moist sponge, rather like a brownie.

100 g plain flour

1 teaspoon baking powder

½ teaspoon bicarbonate of soda

a pinch of salt

60 g good plain chocolate

2 tablespoons cocoa powder

200 g caster sugar

75 ml very hot water

2 large eggs, at room temperature, beaten

175 g unsalted butter, at room temperature, diced

2 tablespoons espresso coffee or dark rum

125 ml sour cream

glaze

85 g plain chocolate, broken up

30 g unsalted butter

4 tablespoons icing sugar, sieved

3 tablespoons espresso coffee (or 2 tablespoons water and 1 tablespoon dark rum)

a daisy tin, a non-stick cake tin, 27 x 18 cm, or a roasting tin, greased

makes one cake

processor mocha fudge cake

Sift the flour, baking powder, bicarbonate of soda and salt onto a sheet of greaseproof paper.

Break up the chocolate and put in a food processor. Add the cocoa and half the sugar. Run the machine until the ingredients form a coarse powder, then, with the machine still running, pour in the hot water through the feed tube.

As soon as the chocolate has melted, pour in the beaten eggs, followed by rest of the sugar. After 30 seconds, stop the machine and scrape down the bowl. Add the butter, process for 1 minute, then stop the machine and scrape down the bowl again. Add the coffee and sour cream and process for a few seconds, just until mixed. Add the flour mixture and process a few seconds more to make a smooth, even batter.

Pour the mixture into the prepared tin, spread it right into the corners, then bake in a preheated oven at 160°C (325°F) Gas 3 for 45–50 minutes until a skewer inserted in the centre comes out clean. Let cool in the tin, then turn out onto a serving platter.

To make the glaze, put the chocolate, butter, icing sugar, coffee (or water and rum) in a small saucepan. Set over the lowest possible heat and stir gently until melted and smooth. Remove from the heat. Leave until thick enough to coat the cake, then pour or spoon over the cake and leave until set.

Store in an airtight container. Best eaten within 4 days.

A truly rich and moist cake made without flour, but with plenty of chocolate.

fudgy pecan cake

350 g good plain chocolate

175 g unsalted butter

50 g cocoa powder, sifted

5 large eggs, at room temperature

250 g caster sugar

100 g pecan nuts, coarsely chopped

icing sugar, for dusting

a daisy tin, a non-stick cake tin, 27 x 18 cm, or a roasting tin, greased

makes one cake

Break up the chocolate and put in a heatproof bowl. Add the butter. Set the bowl over a pan of steaming hot water and melt gently, stirring frequently. Remove the bowl from the pan and stir in the cocoa.

Put the eggs in a large electric mixer and beat well. Add the sugar and whisk on high speed until the mixture is very light, fluffy, and tripled in volume. Remove the bowl from the mixer.

Using a large metal spoon, carefully fold in the chocolate mixture followed by the pecans.

Spoon into the prepared tin and spread evenly. Bake in a preheated oven at 180°C (350°F) Gas 4 for about 30 minutes until the top of the cake is firm, but the centre still slightly soft. Let cool for 10 minutes, then turn out of the tin. Dust with icing sugar and serve at room temperature or warm with whipped cream.

Store in an airtight container and eat within 4 days.

This cake is a simple, all-in-one mixture spiked with fresh orange zest and juice and covered with glaze richly flavoured with fresh orange juice or orange liqueur.

fresh orange cake with sticky glaze

240 g unsalted butter, very soft

240 g caster sugar

4 large eggs

330 g self-raising flour

1 teaspoon baking powder

a pinch of salt

the grated zest and juice of
1 large unwaxed orange

glaze

120 g unsalted butter

70 g caster sugar

5 tablespoons fresh orange juice,
orange liqueur or whisky

*a daisy tin, a non-stick cake tin,
27 x 18 cm, or a roasting tin,
greased*

makes one cake

To make the sponge, put the butter and sugar in a large bowl, then add the eggs, flour, baking powder, salt and orange zest and juice. Beat with a wooden spoon or electric whisk or mixer on low speed for 1 minute until smooth and thoroughly mixed.

Spoon the mixture into the prepared tin and smooth the surface. Bake in a preheated oven at 180°C (350°F) Gas 4 for 40–45 minutes or until a skewer inserted in the centre comes out clean.

Towards the end of the baking time, prepare the glaze. Put the butter, sugar and the 5 tablespoons orange juice in a small saucepan and heat gently until melted. Keep the mixture warm.

When the sponge is cooked, lift it out of the oven but keep it in the tin for 5 minutes. Turn it out onto a serving platter with a slight rim. Prick the cake all over with a skewer. Reheat the glaze, if necessary, and spoon it evenly over the cake. Let cool. Serve at room temperature with whipped cream.

Store in an airtight container and eat within 4 days.

One of the easiest, quickest and prettiest cakes you can make. The all-in-one lemon sponge can be made from scratch in under an hour – the simple fruit topping takes just a couple of minutes to arrange.

citrus summer cake

175 g unsalted butter, softened but not oily

250 g caster sugar

3 large eggs, at room temperature, beaten

250 g self-raising flour

½ teaspoon baking powder

125 ml milk

the grated zest of 2 unwaxed medium lemons

topping

4 tablespoons Lemon Curd (page 62)

2 tablespoons toasted flaked almonds

250 g mixed berries (such as strawberries, raspberries, blueberries, blackberries and redcurrants)

icing sugar, for dusting

a daisy tin, a non-stick cake tin, 27 x 18 cm, or a roasting tin, greased

makes one cake

To make the sponge, put the butter, sugar, eggs, flour, baking powder, milk and lemon zest in an electric mixer. Using medium speed, beat until the mixture is thick and fluffy with no sign of lumps or streaks of flour.

Spoon into the prepared tin and spread evenly. Bake in a preheated oven at 180°C (350°F) Gas 4 for about 30 minutes, or until a skewer inserted in the centre comes out clean. Let cool in the tin for 10 minutes, then turn out onto a wire rack to cool completely. When cold, the cake can be stored in an airtight container for up to 2 days.

When ready to serve, set the cake on a serving platter. Brush the sides and top of the cake with the Lemon Curd, then sprinkle flaked almonds all over it. Arrange the berries on top and around the cake, dust with icing sugar and serve.

Store in an airtight container in the refrigerator and eat within 2 days.

This traditional cake, made with equal weights of butter, sugar, eggs and flour, needs plenty of beating to add air and lightness. Here the work is done with an electric mixer, and the dried berries add a burst of flavour.

blueberry lemon pound cake

250 g unsalted butter, at room temperature

250 g caster sugar

grated zest of 1 large unwaxed lemon

4 large eggs, at room temperature

a pinch of salt

250 g self-raising flour

75 g dried blueberries

icing sugar, for dusting

a daisy tin, a non-stick cake tin, 27 x 18 cm, or a roasting tin, greased

makes one cake

Put the butter in an electric mixer and beat at low speed until creamy. Increase the speed and gradually beat in the sugar, followed by the lemon zest.

Put the eggs and salt in a jug, beat lightly, then add to the creamed mixture, 1 tablespoon or so at a time, beating well after each addition. Add 1 tablespoon flour with the 2 last portions of egg to prevent the mixture from separating.

Sift the rest of the flour onto the mixture and gently fold in with a large metal spoon. When you no longer see streaks of flour, mix in the blueberries.

Transfer to the prepared tin and spread evenly. Bake in a preheated oven at 180°C (350°F) Gas 4 for about 40 minutes or until a skewer inserted in the centre comes out clean. Let cool in the tin for 10 minutes, then carefully turn out onto a wire rack to cool completely. Dust with icing sugar before serving.

Store in an airtight container and eat within 5 days.

Use tart apples for the best flavour – a cooking variety such as Bramley, or Granny Smith all-purpose apples.

apple and walnut honey spice cake

250 ml clear honey

120 g unsalted butter, softened

100 g light muscovado sugar

2 large eggs, beaten

300 g self-raising flour

2 teaspoons ground mixed spice

450 g apples, peeled, cored and chopped

100 g walnut pieces

icing sugar, for dusting

a daisy tin, a non-stick cake tin, 27 x 18 cm, or a roasting tin, greased

makes one cake

Put the honey, butter, sugar and eggs in a large bowl. Sift the flour and mixed spice into the bowl, then stir gently with a wooden spoon or use an electric mixer on low speed. When thoroughly mixed, stir in the apples and walnuts. Transfer to the prepared tin and spread evenly.

Bake in a preheated oven at 180°C (350°F) Gas 4 for 40–50 minutes, until a skewer inserted in the centre of the cake comes out clean. Let cool in the tin for 15 minutes, then turn out onto a wire rack to cool completely.

Dust with icing sugar, then serve warm or at room temperature with whipped cream on the side.

Store in an airtight container and eat within 3 days.

other cakes

A wonderful, rich combination of roasted hazelnuts, light muscovado sugar and thick, dark, chocolate cream.

hazelnut meringue cake

185 g ready-skinned (white) hazelnuts

250 g light muscovado sugar

6 large egg whites

a pinch of salt

chocolate cream

300 g good plain chocolate

385 ml double cream

cocoa powder, grated chocolate or Chocolate Brittle (page 61), for decorating

2 baking trays, lined with non-stick baking parchment

makes one 2-layer cake

Put the nuts in a baking dish and toast in a preheated oven at 150°C (300°F) Gas 2 until they are evenly golden brown, about 10 minutes. Cool, then transfer to a food processor and pulse to make a coarse powder. Reserve 2 tablespoons of the sugar and add the remainder to the food processor. Pulse to mix and set aside.

Put the egg whites and salt in a spotlessly clean, grease-free bowl and whisk with an electric mixer or whisk until soft peaks form. Add the reserved 2 tablespoons sugar, whisking until the meringue is stiff and glossy. Using a large metal spoon, very gently fold in the nut and sugar mixture.

Divide the mixture in half and spoon 1 portion into the centre of each prepared tray. Spread out each portion to a circle about 20 cm across. Bake in the preheated oven at 150°C (300°F) Gas 2 for 1¼–1½ hours until golden, firm and crisp. If necessary, rotate the trays so the meringues cook evenly. Let cool completely, then peel off the paper.

Meanwhile, to make the chocolate cream, break up the chocolate into small squares and put in a food processor. Gently heat the cream until scalding hot but not boiling. With the processor running, pour the cream through the feed tube into the bowl of chocolate. As soon as the mixture has become smooth and thick, turn off the machine. In warm weather, chill until thick enough to spread.

Put a circle of meringue on a serving platter and spread with about one-third of the chocolate cream. Top with the second circle, then quickly cover the top and sides with the rest of the chocolate cream. Chill until ready to serve, then sprinkle with cocoa, grated chocolate or Chocolate Brittle.

The cake can be kept in an airtight container in the refrigerator for up to 3 days.

The best American shortcake is somewhere between an English scone, shortbread and sponge cake, with a crunchy crust and soft, rich, tender crumb. You can try blueberries, blackberries or raspberries instead of strawberries, and lemon juice instead of orange.

strawberry shortcakes

450 g ripe strawberries, hulled

1–2 tablespoons caster sugar, to taste

2 tablespoons fresh orange juice

shortcake

250 g self-raising flour, plus extra for working

a large pinch of salt

½ teaspoon baking powder

the grated zest 1 unwaxed orange

80 g caster sugar, plus extra for sprinkling

80 g unsalted butter, chilled and diced

about 230 ml whipping cream, chilled

30 g unsalted butter, softened, for brushing

a large bowl whipped cream, for serving

a 7.5 cm plain round biscuit cutter

a baking tray, greased

makes 6

Thickly slice the strawberries into a bowl. Sprinkle with the sugar and juice, then mix gently. Cover and leave at room temperature.

Put the flour, salt, baking powder, orange zest and sugar in a food processor and blend for 5 seconds until just mixed. Add the butter and process until the mixture looks like breadcrumbs. With the machine running, pour the cream through the feed tube and mix until the dough comes together to form a soft but not sticky ball.

Carefully remove the dough from the processor and put on a lightly floured work surface. Flour your hands and pat out the dough until it is a good 2.5 cm thick. Cut out rounds using the biscuit cutter, gently kneading the trimmings and patting them out again, to give 6 rounds in all.

Set the rounds slightly apart on the prepared tray and sprinkle the tops with a little sugar. Bake in a preheated oven at 220°C (425°F) Gas 7 for 10 minutes. Reduce to 180°C (350°F) Gas 4 and cook for a further 10 minutes until the shortcakes are firm and golden.

Remove the tray from the oven and brush the tops of the cakes with very soft butter. Let cool on the tray. When firm and completely cooled, split the cakes in half horizontally, but leave in pairs.

When ready to serve, gently warm the shortcakes for 5 minutes in a preheated oven at 180°C (350°F) Gas 4. Transfer to a serving platter and fill the shortcakes with whipped cream, berries and juice. Replace the 'lids' and put a few extra slices of berries on top. Serve immediately with whipped cream. Best eaten the same day.

A pure white cake made with a dozen egg whites. The easiest way to separate whites from yolks is to use eggs straight from the refrigerator, but for best results leave the whites at room temperature for 30 minutes before whisking.

angel's cloud

75 g plain flour

25 g cornflour

a pinch of salt

250 g caster sugar

12 large egg whites

1 teaspoon cream of tartar

the finely grated zest of 1 unwaxed lemon

topping

225 ml double cream, chilled

4 tablespoons Lemon Curd (page 62)

450 g strawberries or blueberries

a rubber spatula

an angel food tin, 25 cm x 10 cm deep, ungreased

makes one large cake

Sift the flour, cornflour, salt and 80 g of the sugar 3 times into a bowl.

Put the egg whites into a spotlessly clean, grease-free bowl and whisk with an electric mixer or whisk on medium speed until fluffy. Add the cream of tartar and lemon zest, then whisk on high speed just until stiff peaks start to form. Whisk in the remaining sugar, 1 tablespoon at a time. Using a large metal spoon or rubber spatula, gently fold in the sifted flour mixture in 3 batches.

Spoon the mixture into the pan and spread evenly with a rubber spatula. Gently tap the pan on the work surface to dislodge any large air pockets. Bake in a preheated oven* at 160°C (325°F) Gas 3 for about 45 minutes until golden and the sponge springs back when gently pressed. Let set and cool completely in the pan – the best way to do this is to invert the pan onto the neck of a funnel or bottle. With a non-stick pan, invert the pan onto a raised wire rack and let cool before gently twisting and lifting off the pan.

Meanwhile to make the topping, whip the cream until soft peaks form, then gently stir in the Lemon Curd.

Carefully unmould the cake and set on a serving platter. Cover with the lemon cream and decorate with berries. Serve immediately or store in an airtight container in the refrigerator and eat within 24 hours. Use a serrated bread knife for cutting.

Manufacturers of some angel food tins recommend a lower temperature or reduced cooking time – refer to manufacturer's guidelines before use. For this cake, it is important to use an ungreased pan – the idea is to get the brown crust to stick to the pan after baking, leaving a white cake. This will not happen with a non-stick pan.

A traditional yet simple sponge cake from France, flavoured with ground almonds. Serve with tea or coffee, or for pudding with fruit salad, cherries or berries and cream.

french almond cake

110 g unsalted butter, softened

150 g caster sugar

3 large eggs, beaten

90 g ground almonds

40 g self-raising flour

1 tablespoon milk or kirsch

1 tablespoon flaked almonds, for sprinkling

icing sugar, for dusting

a sandwich tin, 20 cm diameter, greased and base-lined

makes one cake

Put the butter, sugar and eggs in a large bowl, add the almonds, flour and milk, then beat with an electric mixer or whisk. When quite light and fluffy, spoon into the prepared tin and spread evenly. Sprinkle the flaked almonds over the top.

Bake in a preheated oven at 180°C (350°F) Gas 4 for 30–35 minutes or until the sponge just springs back when pressed. Run a round-bladed knife around the inside edge of the tin to loosen the sponge, then turn out onto a wire rack and let cool. Dust with icing sugar before serving.

Store in an airtight tin and eat within 5 days.

toppings
and sauces

toffee topping

130 g light muscovado sugar

110 g unsalted butter

50 ml whipping cream

½ teaspoon real vanilla extract

Put the sugar, butter and cream in a small saucepan and heat gently until melted. Bring to the boil, then simmer for 3 minutes until thick and toffee-like. Pour into a heatproof bowl and let cool. Stir in the vanilla. Store, tightly covered in the refrigerator for up to 1 week.

toffee sauce

Make the topping above, adding an extra 50 ml cream. Serve warm.

chocolate fudge sauce

175 g plain chocolate, chopped

40 g unsalted butter

2 tablespoons caster sugar

2 tablespoons golden syrup

175 ml single cream

Put all the ingredients in a small, heavy-based saucepan and set over low heat. Stir gently until melted and smooth. Continue heating and stirring until the mixture is almost at boiling point. Remove from the heat and serve. This sauce can be stored, tightly covered in the refrigerator, for up to 4 days.

white chocolate sauce

200 g best-quality white chocolate, chopped

75 ml milk

200 ml double cream

Gently melt the chocolate in a heatproof bowl set over a pan of steaming water. Remove the bowl from the heat and stir gently until smooth. Gently heat the milk and cream until almost boiling, then gently pour onto the chocolate in a thin stream, whisking constantly to make a smooth sauce. Serve.

maple pecan sauce

2 small sweet apples

150 ml maple syrup

50 g pecan halves

Wash the apples and peel only if the skin is very tough and tasteless. Quarter and core the apples and chop into small dice. Put in a medium saucepan with the maple syrup and nuts and heat gently. Serve immediately.

cinnamon cream

Omit the vanilla and add ½ teaspoon ground cinnamon with the sugar.

maple cream

Omit the vanilla and replace the sugar with 1½ teaspoons maple sugar.

crème chantilly

French sweet whipped cream.

225 ml double cream

½ teaspoon vanilla essence

1½ tablespoons caster sugar

If possible, chill the bowl and whisk in the refrigerator or freezer for 30–60 minutes. Pour the cream into the chilled bowl and whip until it starts to thicken. Add the vanilla and sugar and whip again until soft peaks form – take care not to overwhip the cream, or it will separate.

chocolate brittle

An easy decoration – melt good-quality plain chocolate and pour onto a baking tray lined with non-stick baking paper. Spread thinly. The chocolate can be left plain or sprinkled with sliced nuts. Leave to set in a cool place then break up and use to decorate cakes.

fresh raspberry preserve

The cheat's recipe for a vibrant, soft-set conserve. Because the fruit is not cooked, choose dry, almost-ripe berries and sugar-with-pectin (the type sold for jam and jelly making), and store this preserve in the refrigerator or freezer. Use as a filling, topping or sauce for plain cakes.

225 g sugar-with-pectin or caster sugar

500 g raspberries or strawberries,
at room temperature

2 tablespoons freshly squeezed lemon juice

makes about 675 g

Put the sugar in a heatproof bowl (non-aluminium) and warm in a low oven 150°C (300°F) Gas 2 for 10 minutes. Meanwhile, crush the fruit with a potato masher or fork. Mix the fruit into the warm sugar and stir very well. Leave the bowl in a warm, sunny spot for 1 hour, stirring occasionally to dissolve the sugar. Stir in the lemon juice, then spoon the mixture into freezer-proof containers. Cover and leave in a cool spot overnight.

Next day, gently stir the preserve. Chill in the refrigerator for 1–2 days until thickened, then use immediately or freeze for up to 6 months. Defrost in the refrigerator and use immediately.

lemon curd

110 g unsalted butter

230 g caster sugar

the grated zest and juice of
2 large or 3 medium unwaxed lemons

3 large eggs, beaten

makes about 500 g

Put the butter, sugar and lemon zest and juice in the top of a non-aluminium double saucepan or in a saucepan set in a roasting tin of boiling water. Set the double pan or roasting tin over medium heat, so the water boils gently. Cook the butter mixture, stirring constantly with a wooden spoon, until smooth and melted. Add the eggs and stir until the mixture becomes very thick and opaque – avoid short cuts, because if the mixture boils, the eggs will scramble. Spoon into clean jars. When completely cold, use or cover and store in the refrigerator for up to 2 weeks.

mango sauce

flesh of 2 large ripe mangoes

freshly squeezed juice of ½ lime

sugar, to taste (optional)

Put the mango flesh and lime juice in a blender or food processor. Purée until very smooth. Taste, then add another squeeze of lime or a spoonful of sugar as necessary. Serve immediately or cover tightly and store in the refrigerator for up to 2 days. Use with daisy cakes or mini Bundts.

melba sauce

500 g raspberries, fresh or frozen and thawed

icing sugar, to taste

Purée the fruit in a processor or blender. Add sugar to taste (depending on the tartness of the fruit and your own preference). Process for 1 minute more to make sure the sugar has dissolved. The sauce can be served as it is or strained through a sieve to remove the seeds. Serve immediately or cover and store in the refrigerator for up to 2 days. Use with daisy cakes or mini Bundts.

mail order and websites

Cucina Direct
PO BOX 6611
London SW15 2WG
Tel: 0870 420 4300
www.cucinadirect.co.uk
*Interesting selection of mail
order baking and kitchen
equipment, including Bundt
tins. Telephone for a
catalogue or browse online.*

David Mellor
4 Sloane Square
London SW1 8EE
Tel: 020 7730 4259
www.davidmellordesign.co.uk
*Well-stocked shop with all
the bakeware you'll ever
need, including Bundt tins.
Mail order available.*

Divertimenti
139–141 Fulham Road
London SW3 6SD
Tel: 020 7581 8066
33–34 Marylebone
High Street
London W1U 4PT
Tel: 020 7935 0689
www.divertimenti.co.uk
*Two shops in London selling
a fine range of kitchen
equipment, including Bundt
tins, plus comprehensive mail
order catalogue.*

Lakeland Limited
Alexandra Buildings
Windermere
Cumbria LA23 1BQ
Tel: 015394 88100
www.lakelandlimited.com
*Huge range of high quality,
good value, cooking
equipment, including Bundt
tins, cake liners, and some
hard-to-find ingredients.
Available from their many
shops and also from their
legendary fast and friendly
mail order service (phone
for a catalogue), as well
as online.*

NordicWare
www.nordicware.com
*Shaped Bundt tins are made
by NordicWare, and are
available from cookshops,
department stores and by
mail order. For more details
contact NordicWare online.*

Silverwood Limited
Ledsam House
Ledsam Street
Birmingham B16 8DN
Tel: 0121 454 3571/2
sales@alan-silverwood.co.uk
*Makers of professional
quality bakeware – cake tins,
loaf tins, baking trays,
rectangular tins, etc. Stocked
by John Lewis, Lakeland, big
department stores and good
cookshops. Phone or email
for details of your local
stockists.*

index